SELLING YOUR PROPERTY IN MASSACHUSETTS

HOW TO SELL ON TIME, REDUCE YOUR RISK, AND MOVE ON TO YOUR NEXT PROPERTY

By David R. Rocheford, Jr., Esq.

ISBN: 978-1-941645-26-0

REALTOR® is a federally registered collective membership mark which identifies a real estate professional who is a Member of the NATIONAL ASSOCIATION OF REALTORS® and subscribes to its strict Code of Ethics.

3rd Edition 2019

DISCLAIMER

This publication is intended to be informational only. No legal advice is being given, and no attorney-client relationship is intended to be created by reading this material. If you are facing legal issues, whether criminal or civil, seek professional legal counsel to get your questions answered.

The Law Office of David R. Rocheford, Jr., P.C.
156 Hamilton Street
Leominster, MA 01453
(978) 728-5104
www.TheBestClosings.com

With great thanks
to my loving wife Danielle
and to my team

Contents

Introduction

I have been involved in real estate transactions for the past twenty years and personally represented thousands of sellers, buyers and mortgage lenders. From that, I've built a law practice, particularly efficient at handling real estate matters. It only made sense to me to take some of that experience and share it with potential clients and industry professionals in this book.

This book is written with the expectation that you, the reader, are considering the sale of, or are in the process of selling, your home (or other real estate).

Understand that an attorney does not have to represent or be involved in a real estate transaction on behalf of the seller. It solely depends on the seller's comfort level, level of experience, and the amount of time they can dedicate to the demands of the transaction. But the importance of having an attorney is stressed, as it can bring peace of mind for all parties involved.

Therefore, sellers are advised to accurately assess and determine their understanding of the legal matters pertaining to their transaction. Even the smallest of errors or oversight can complicate a simple transaction and needlessly delay the completion of a transaction. Nothing agitates me more than needless delays in real estate transactions.

You are welcome to contact me to discuss any of the material herein or if you have questions about your particular real estate transaction.

David

The Importance of Your Team

As with every important endeavor, there will always be risks involved, especially when it comes to selling your home. You can, however, take measures to reduce the risks by hiring professionals to help you in the process of selling your property and look out for your best interests.

I cannot stress enough the importance of working with professionals who you know, like, and trust. I have seen more real estate transactions fall apart due to a poor choice of professionals representing the parties. On choosing the right professionals to assist you, first keep it local. Work with professionals in your community. They know the market, customs and practices. Second, work with experienced individuals. They can draw on their experience in circumstances where only experience provides the best options. Third, communication is such a crucial part of a successful transaction that you want to work with someone who has the means and availability to communicate with everyone involved in the transaction.

Your team should be comprised of at least two integral members, both performing unique tasks pertaining to their specialty. These will be your real estate agent and your real estate attorney. Remember, when looking for legal services for your real estate transaction, you will want to make sure your attorney has significant experience and knowledge in handling real estate matters.

Your real estate agent will take care of pricing, presenting, marketing your property to ensure maximum exposure and getting the highest possible price and most qualified buyer. They will also deal with the negotiations and work towards a speedy closing of the deal. I'll address this more in a later section of this book.

The Seller's Attorney

While it is true that hiring the services of a real estate attorney can increase the cost of your transaction, it is money well spent. The cost associated with a real estate attorney, who will represent you, will vary depending on the particulars of the transaction and the attorney you decide to hire. However, I always encourage my clients to find an attorney who uses a flat fee schedule for their services. This allows you to reduce the uncertainty regarding the final cost of the service.

Role of a Real Estate Attorney

Retaining the services of an experienced attorney allows a seller to be able to anticipate potential problems relating to their transactions before they become actual problems. Only an attorney, experienced in real estate matters, will be able to detect minor issues in advance, and address them before any serious and potentially costly problems result.

It is best to retain the legal counsel of an attorney as early as possible in the transaction. Waiting until the last minute to hire an attorney, or after a problem occurs, will most likely end up costing more for the same service.

The most important and time intensive part of a transaction is becoming familiar with the parties and the facts of a transaction. So, whether I am retained by a seller at the start of a transaction, or in the middle, after a problem occurs, I still need to get familiar with the parties and the facts. Then

I have to address the problem. However, when I am retained at the start, I can often identify and avoid issues, before they become problems.

The Written Agreements

Technically, a written contract is not a mandatory requirement. You could conceivably have someone walk up to you, hand you $200,000 and sign over the deed. Obviously, the deed has to be in writing and recorded as part of the public record, which is a legal requirement. But, there is no particular need to have a written agreement between the buyer and seller.

However, any agreement involving the sale of real estate that is not in writing is unenforceable. If one of the parties violates the agreement (you sign over the deed and the buyer says they will only give you $150,000), the seller would have no recourse because the court won't enforce a verbal agreement for the sale of real estate. Every material detail of the agreement between the buyer and the seller has to be in writing and signed by both of the parties involved.

If both parties cooperate and there are no breaches in the verbal agreement, then they could just go right to the closing and there would be no problem. The only time an issue comes up is if there is a matter of enforcement of the contract, which can obviously, only be enforced if there is hard evidence of the agreement, i.e. a written contract.

The seller most often provides the initial purchase and sale agreement to the buyer. A real estate agent may assist in filling out a standard form agreement, but it is in the seller's best interest to have the agreement prepared by a qualified attorney. Once the agreement is prepared it is provided to the buyer for review and signatures. Often, a buyer will retain their own attorney to review the agreement. The buyer's attorney may request changes, or edits to the initial agreement. Those changes or edits, if not understood, should be reviewed by the seller's attorney.

Transfer of Property

Customarily, it is the seller's responsibility to provide the new deed transferring, or conveying, ownership from the seller to the buyer. The deed is a legal document and should be drafted by a qualified attorney. In fact, the buyer's attorney, or the attorney for the buyer's mortgage lender may not accept a deed that has not been prepared by an attorney. A poorly drafted deed can critically affect the chain of title and cause problems for the buyer during their ownership. The attorney's fee for preparing the deed is the responsibility of the seller, unless otherwise agreed between the buyer and seller.

Addressing Liens and Title Issues

The buyer's attorney, or the attorney for the buyer's mortgage lender will conduct an examination of the chain of ownership of the property prior to closing. This is referred to as the title exam. The closing attorney will use the title exam to determine ownership and what actions or procedures will be necessary to transfer ownership from the seller to the buyer.

The title exam will reveal any outstanding mortgages, court judgments, encumbrances or other liens that must be satisfied by the seller prior to closing. If the report shows discrepancies in the chain of title the seller will be responsible for resolving the problems. A discrepancy is often referred to as "title defect"; "cloud on title" or simply a "title issue".

As a seller's attorney, I often assist my clients with resolving title defects. I address this in more detail in a later section of this book.

The Real Estate Agent and Broker

Many people looking to sell their properties attempt to cut costs by not using the services of a real estate agent. Although, the task is not entirely impossible to achieve without the expert services of a real estate agent, the seller should be willing and prepared to take on a lot of legwork required to manage the entire selling process without any discrepancies, all of this without any real guarantee of a final sale.

Before making a decision of working with a real estate agent or not, the seller should at least ask themselves the following questions and answer them honestly:

1. Am I aware of the actual value of the property in the current market?

2. Will I be willing and ready to work with the buyer's real estate agent?

3. Will I be able to effectively take care of all the responsibilities associated with the marketing of the property and its eventual sale?

4. Will I be able to bear the impending criticism of my home after the buyer's inspection?

5. Am I willing and able to screen all potential buyers?

If you, as a seller, have honestly answered yes to all of these questions, then you are at least willing to take on the work involved in the sale of a property. Despite your willingness, you cannot accurately assess your understanding of the processes involved in the sale of a property, so tread with caution.

Selling a Home is Easy – Right?

The most common misconception has to be the notion that it's easy to sell your property on your own. You just put your home on the market, have someone make you an offer, and close 30 days later. However, it doesn't really work like that, at least not in reality. The process is quite extensive and intricate and there are a number of variables that, if not handled perfectly, can make the process go very wrong.

There are many players involved in this process. First, you have the buyer and seller; the buyer's attorney and the seller's attorney; the real estate agents, and then there are the families of both the seller and the buyer. There is obviously a lot of emotion on both sides. More about emotions later.

Then you have those players who are involved in an indirect capacity, including the lenders, the loan officers, the appraisers and the home inspectors. All of these people play a vital role in the transaction. Having so many personalities involved in a transaction only serves to complicate matters even further. There is no particular standard or cookie cutter type of transaction that a person can employ. This is because every transaction is as unique as the property and no two are ever the same.

Difference between a Real Estate Agent/Broker and a Realtor®

Many people are unfamiliar with the real estate industry and its various terms and jargon. So it is no surprise that many people use the term Realtor®, real estate agent and broker interchangeably, which essentially is incorrect.

A Realtor® is the term used to refer to a real estate agent who has become a member of the National Association of Realtors®. This means, the agent is bound by the associations' professional standards and its code of ethics. The association attempts to standardize the real estate industry by introducing high standards for its agents and ensure that clients don't have to worry if their agent represents their best interests or not.

A real estate agent is a professional who has undertaken all of the necessary classes and passed their licensing exam to acquire the license required to become a real estate agent. Each state has its own licensing body, requirements and testing, which a person must take in order to work as a real estate agent in that particular state.

A real estate broker has ventured even further in terms of real estate education and has passed the broker license exam. A broker's license allows an agent to work independently of another broker or even hire other agents to work for them.

The distinction here is that a real estate agent has to work through a real estate broker who would be responsible for overseeing their actions and providing guidance and resources whenever necessary. A Realtor®, on the other hand, has been able to acquire membership of a prestigious association that further attests their competency and ethical responsibilities. Whenever possible, I recommend working with a real estate agent or broker who is a Realtor®. That being said, there are many outstanding and qualified real estate agents and brokers who are not Realtors® and they do a fine job for their clients.

Pricing

One of the main things to take into consideration when selling your property is the pricing. If the property is not priced correctly, it will sit on the market for an extended period of time. If you end up pricing your property too high, your property will most certainly languish on the market. Obviously, when a property sits on the market for a long time, potential buyers will no doubt wonder about the condition or any other issues that are preventing the property from selling. Sellers often underestimate the actual value of market time and the impact it has on perceived value.

Despite what it may seem to a non-professional, pricing of a property requires considerable amount of knowledge and experience. It also requires thorough understanding of the market and its prevailing trends along with the inventory and its condition. A lot people believe that online pricing services have made it quite easy to price a property, but think about it. You cannot expect a service to price your property without properly examining it, and without adequate knowledge of the details of your particular market. So, such online services are best used to get a perspective price range or value, and not for setting the asking pricing. You will need a professional agent specializing in your market to be able to accurately price your property.

Property Marketing

Although, it may be easy to advertise your home on the internet these days, it still takes considerable amounts of skill and experience to advertise it properly. A real estate agent is trained to know what medium works in a particular market and for a particular property type. In fact, advertising your property in the wrong location or using the wrong medium can dramatically affect the outcome of your transaction.

Every market has one or two agents, or brokers, who have a reputation for being able to move a particular style of property effectively. Can you get your property in front of those agents on your own? An agent working for you will know where, and to whom to market the property.

Understand All of the Processes Involved in a Real Estate Transaction

Many details can be overlooked in the process of selling real estate, and an experienced agent understands the process better than someone who lacks experience performing the task. For example, a seller may not realize the need for certain inspections and legal processes that have to be performed before listing or closing. And if the buyer and the bank have an attorney, the seller is expected to know the process and do all that is required of them.

On so many occasions, while serving as the closing attorney, I have seen sellers completely unprepared to close on schedule because they have overlooked an elementary step in the process.

Be Willing to Work with the Buyer's Agent

If the buyer and the lender have acquired the services of an attorney, they will be asking you questions that you may not be able to answer unless you're familiar with the process and understand all of the intricacies of the sale of real estate.

If a buyer's agent brings you a potential buyer, you will likely be obligated to pay the buyer's agent a commission. However, the buyer's agent is just that, an agent for the buyer. The agent will have little fiduciary duty to you as the seller.

Refusing to work with, and pay a buyer's agent will significantly reduce your pool of potential buyers. Even if you do offer to pay a buyer agent fee, some buyer agents will avoid properties advertised for sale by the owner. This is because such transactions are inherently burdensome and the buyer agent ends up doing far more work than they expected to do.

The Emotional Aspect of Selling Real Estate

All forms of transactions that involve large sums of money automatically invoke a person's emotions. One of the first things that investors of all sorts learn is that they must control their emotions over a transaction. This is particularly true when someone is selling their home.

Unlike a homeowner, a real estate agent can easily follow up on the details of a transaction without exuding a sense of eagerness or desperation. After all, following up is a huge part of their job. For example, when a homeowner repeatedly checks with a potential buyer, they give off the appearance they are willing to accept a lower price or that they are not confident – a true impediment in the negotiation process.

Moreover, who wouldn't take offense at hearing negative remarks at the place they've called home for years. Having an agent will shield you from the nastiness of rejection and present them in the form of creative criticism, which is much easier to digest.

Here are a few signs that you may be letting your emotions affect your transaction:

- You ignore the "comps" or comparable properties because you feel that the particular comp property is in no way comparable to yours.

- You ignore your agent's advice about staging the property and about having it in a particular condition for showings.

- You become overly sensitive during negotiating price, repairs, and other contract details.

- You refuse to re-evaluate your position when conditions like days on market, buyer feedback, or other influences would indicate that it would be prudent to reevaluate your current strategy.

Investing Time

When you put your property on the market, potential buyers will contact you to see the property at times convenient for them. This will require you to rush home every time someone wants to see the property. If selling your home is not your fulltime job, you will be forced to excuse yourself from work or meetings every time a potential buyer calls. Even if you schedule all of the showings after work, would you be able to continue this day after day? A real estate agent, on the other hand, will be available whenever there is an opportunity to show the property or anything else that would require time and effort.

Professional Eyes

An agent has been trained in the art of presentation. They know exactly how to present a property in order for it to appeal to someone who is looking to buy. Their professional expertise will help the seller to make necessary changes to attract buyers and get the best possible offers. They will be able to see the flaws that a seller would consider to be its strengths. Their professional experience and training will allow the home to sell much quicker on the market at the best possible rate.

Statistically, it's been shown that properties sell for substantially less without the assistance of a real estate agent involved in the transaction. This is because they know about effective marketing techniques, pricing, negotiating and preparing or staging the property in a way to make sure it appeals to potential buyers.

The Costs of Selling a Home

Selling a property can be an exhilarating and fantastic experience, especially if you bought the property below market value and will have sizeable profits. However, the same experience can also be quite disappointing and distressing if you stand to lose money from the transaction. Even a property bought at a low price can end up with little or no profits and in the worst case end up costing you. This is particularly true if you are not aware of all the various costs involved in the process of selling a property.

Because there are many different costs incurred in the process of selling a house, having a good understanding of those costs before making the decision to sell can make the entire experience much more enjoyable. Unexpected costs always seem to ruin an otherwise pleasant transaction. That's why it's particularly important for you to be aware of all of the costs involved in a real estate transaction to make sound and educated decisions.

This section covers some of the costs you will be responsible for at the time of closing.

Brokerage Commissions

The most common and obvious cost for sellers is the commission associated with the real estate brokerage.

Commissions tend to be variable, running between two and six percent of the sale price depending on the transaction. Commissions are negotiated up front with the real estate broker, prior to listing the property. Although the commission is based off of the final sale price there are circumstances, such as providing a buyer credit, which may affect the seller's net proceeds. For example, if the agent negotiates a buyer credit of $5,000 to cover closing costs and the sale price is increased from $200,000 to $205,000 the commission should be based off the initial price of $200,000 and not off of $205,000.

Attorney Fees

A seller's attorney's fees typically run between $125 and $900, depending on the amount of work the attorney has to do for the seller. However, it is not uncommon for that number to go a lot higher depending on the circumstances of the transaction, as complicated cases or legal issues will require a lot more work on the attorney's part, resulting in heftier legal fees.

Recording Fees and Excise Tax

Recording fees are associated with the recording of the required documents with the registry of deeds, which usually ranges around $200-300. Each document is assessed a recording fee and the fee varies depending on the type of document and references that the documents makes. There may also be a surcharge fee of some sort for recording documents electronically. Such a fee is around $5 per document. The most common document a seller will pay to record is a mortgage discharge, which is currently about $75.

In the state of Massachusetts, we have a real estate excise tax or sales tax, which is often referred to as tax stamps, and it's based on the sale price of the property, with the rate being $4.56 per thousand of the sale price. The tax is collected from the seller by the closing attorney and paid to the State when the deed is recorded. It only applies when the sale price is greater than $99.

Don't overlook the cost of this tax. It is one of the most unexpected costs I see sellers face at closing.

Title Insurance and Buyer Credits

Title insurance in Massachusetts is commonly paid by the buyer, so the seller is usually not responsible for that expense. However, there are occasions where the seller assumes this cost as part of negotiations with the buyer.

A common seller concession in a transaction is to give the buyer a credit for some or all of the buyers closing costs. Aptly referred to as a buyer closing cost credit. So, if this is something you have agreed to you can expect that it will be accounted for at the closing. It will appear on the settlement statement as a line item credit and it reduces the seller's proceeds by the amount of the credit.

Mortgage Payoffs

There are also mortgage payoffs to consider. If you currently have a mortgage on the property being sold, you will be required to pay off the entire mortgage at the closing. This can include various fees such as early payment fee, past due fees, statement fees and escrow account shortages.

Either the closing attorney or the seller's attorney will obtain the current balance information and use it to calculate the total amount due for paying off each outstanding mortgage. The payoff will be calculated a few days beyond the closing date. This takes into account possible delays in the delivery of the funds to the lien holder or the lender. A payoff figure will be required for any type of lien against the property. This includes Home Equity Lines of Credit (HELOCs), even if they have a zero balance.

Prior to listing the property for sale, a seller should have an accurate idea of the estimated amount necessary to pay off the mortgage. If the seller does not have an accurate estimation of the payoff amount, it can possibly lead to a situation where the sale price would prove to be insufficient to satisfy the mortgage and all of the other expenses related to the transaction.

In such a case, you would be obligated to bring money to the closing in order to complete the sale. In the worst case scenario, you would need to negotiate a short sale with your current lender.

If the current lender has an escrow account for the homeowner insurance and/or the real estate taxes, the resulting balance will also have to be accounted for in the figure determined for the payoff. Otherwise, any remaining escrow funds will be returned to you after the closing is completed.

Another important thing to note is that, the mortgage payoff amount will never be the total principal amount shown as due on the most recent statement, but rather it would also include the per diem (daily) interest for the remaining period between the due date and the actual receipt of the payment.

Municipal Real Estate Taxes

Municipal real estate taxes for the property for the current tax period will be accounted for at closing. Any outstanding taxes, the interest and administrative fees, for a previous tax period will also have to be paid at the time of the closing.

Because most municipal real estate taxes are paid in advance, typically in the middle of the period, the seller will receive a credit (or adjustment) from the buyer for reimbursement of taxes paid in advance. If the taxes due for a current period are unpaid, the seller will likely owe the buyer a credit for the seller's portion of the tax period.

Adjustments to pay for municipal services such as water and sewer services, trash disposal and other similar municipal services, will be accounted for at the closing. These adjustments should also be considered when you estimate the municipalexpenses.

Miscellaneous Costs

Although, the costs at closing are reasonably easy to anticipate and calculate, there will be miscellaneous costs accounted for at closing. These costs are usually the result of circumstances that arise between the signing of the purchase and sale contract and the actual closing, such as credits for repairs and services rendered to the seller to effectuate the closing.

The Process of Selling a Home

Despite hiring a real estate agent and an attorney to represent seller interests in the real estate transaction, it is important for the seller to be well acquainted with the entire process. This understanding will ensure that, the seller feels confident in their decision and all the choices they will have to make. This section covers some of the most important steps involved in selling your property.

Prepare for the Transition

When you decide to sell your home, you will obviously need another place to stay, as you simply cannot proceed towards the closing without vacating the place. This is something we will discuss in detail in a following section.

Decide whether you will be renting for a while or you have already found another property you wish to call home. Whichever the case maybe, you need to figure this out and the resulting expenses will be added to your overall personal costs. You don't want to be left unprepared when you manage to find a decent offer.

The Offer to Purchase and Purchase and Sale Agreement

So, you have your real estate agent and your attorney and your house on the market. Now, you will have to wait for a potential buyer to make an offer on the property. Hopefully, this will happen sooner than later. When it does, the offer will contain the basic terms of the transaction, including the offer price, the initial deposits the buyer will make, and dates regarding the transaction, as well as, a list of personal property and appliances to be included or excluded in the deal.

If you are satisfied with the terms of the offer, you have the option to accept it. Of course, you also have the option of countering the offer if you are dissatisfied with the terms. This allows the buyer and seller to go on and negotiate the terms of the deal.

You want to be certain that the offer contains provisions and contingencies that are important to you and your circumstances. An example would be a contingency for the purchase of a new home or your satisfactory relocation before a certain date. Nothing prohibits you from being creative with the terms of the offer provided the terms are acceptable to the buyer, as well.

The bottom line is, once the offer or counter offer is accepted, the next step is initiated to move on to the finalization of the purchase and sale agreement, which is a bit like the offer. However, it contains a lot more detail, including specific dates and milestones, remedies in case of a breach of contract, and contingencies for the buyer and seller. For example, the buyer's performance under the terms of the agreement may be contingent upon obtaining mortgage financing and upon the completion of all necessary inspections before the transaction can be completed.

As mentioned earlier, it is customarily the seller's responsibility to produce the first draft of the agreement. A real estate agent can assist in filling out a standard form agreement. The purchase and sale agreement should mirror the terms of the offer and contain all of the material terms of the offer unless otherwise agreed upon.

Home Inspection

Although, it's not mandatory, a buyer will usually have a professional home inspection conducted on the property. The inspection is often completed prior to entering into a purchase and sale agreement, but occasionally the purchase and sale agreement will be signed prior to the inspection. In that event, there will likely be a contingency for the completion of the inspection included as a term of the agreement.

If the buyer's home inspection discloses issues that the buyer is not satisfied with, the buyer is entitled to the return of their deposit. Issues can vary from minor defects, like inoperative systems, broken fixtures, to critical issues such as termite infestation or structural defects. Inspections sometimes include testing for radon, mold, and water quality and quantity to list a few.

The buyer may negotiate with you to address the issues that were disclosed by the inspection. Some of the options you may have in that kind of negotiation are:

- Repair some or all of the issues on your own;

- Hire a professional to complete some or all of the repairs;

- Reduce the sale price by an estimated cost of the repairs;

- Provide the buyer with a credit for the estimated cost of the repairs.

- Return the buyer's deposit and find a new buyer.

Extension or Termination

If all goes according to plan, the next step would be to move on and prepare for the closing process. In the event that the buyer is unable to get their inspections done in the allotted time, they may ask the seller for an extension of the time to complete it. The purchase and sale agreement will likely contain a contingency provision for the buyer to obtain mortgage financing. Similarly, if the buyer is unable to get their financing by a certain date, which is a common occurrence, they may ask the seller for an extension of the financing commitment. The seller can either agree to extend the date, or return the deposit to the buyer and proceed with the termination of the contract and look for other potential buyers. Usually, a mortgage contingency clause will expire two or three weeks prior to the closing.

The Process of Closing

"Closing" is a term used among real estate professionals, and it refers to the completion of a real estate transaction. A closing occurs when parties involved sign their respective documents, and tender the funds, indicating that a transfer of property ownership has been finalized.

Title Examination

Prior to closing, the closing attorney will perform a title examination to ensure that the seller is the true, legal, owner of the property and able to convey the property as agreed. The title exam will also disclose any encumbrances or discrepancies in the title. And the exam will show all outstanding mortgages and liens that the seller must pay off or discharge at closing. The concept of the title, or evidence of ownership, is not unique to Massachusetts. It is essentially the legal standard used throughout the country.

However, Massachusetts' records of the ownership of land go back hundreds of years and they show the various owners of the property over that time. Since Massachusetts has an incredibly long and rich history as a state, it is quite rare to see just two or three former owners of a property. In many cases, the chain of ownership can consist of as many as 10 to 20 owners since the inception of the record. The attorney will examine the chain of title making sure to find any possible discrepancies by looking for title issues such as unexpected encumbrances or liens.

If there are issues disclosed by the examination, it is the seller's responsibility to rectify the issues. An experienced real estate attorney will likely be needed to assist with the resolution of most complex title issues.

Buyer's Walkthrough

In most circumstances, the buyer will have the right to conduct a walkthrough of the property to view the condition and ensure that the property is being delivered as agreed. It is important for the buyer to understand that this is not an opportunity to conduct another inspection of the property. If the buyer has issues with the result of the walkthrough the closing should be delayed until the issues can be addressed. Although, other options are often proposed, it is always in the seller's best interest to delay the closing rather than to commence negotiations with the buyer at the closing table under pressure.

Physical Closing

At the time of the closing, it is a necessity for the seller to be physically present at the closing. In the case that you are unable to attend or simply do not wish to be present at the closing, you may appoint someone to act under the power of an attorney as your legal representative.

However, even if you legally appoint a representative through the power of attorney to act in your place, you will likely be required to execute the new deed personally. If you do not expect to attend the closing, you will have to arrange to sign the relevant documents in advance to ensure the smooth closing. You will also need to arrange for the delivery of your proceeds from the sale. The closing attorney is responsible for disbursement of funds and will pay the seller with a trust account check or electronic wire.

On the other hand, if you are purchasing another property on the same day as the sale and would require the proceeds from the sale to facilitate the purchase, you will have to make sure to coordinate with the closing attorney in advance.

As far as the proceeds of the sale are concerned, you will receive your funds once the new deed has been recorded, which would occur immediately after the closing. You will also have to arrange in advance for how you intend to receive the funds. Again, having your funds electronically wired is the most convenient option, but you can also arrange for the attorney to have a check payable to the closing attorney handling the next transaction, if you are purchasing a new property.

Keys and Access

Once the closing is completed, the deed has been recorded, and the proceeds disbursed, the buyer is entitled to access the property. Arrangements should be made at the closing for the delivery of the keys to the new homeowner; this includes garage door openers and any security alarm codes, if applicable.

I strongly discourage allowing the buyer final access to the property prior to the receipt of proceeds and or the recording of the deed. This situation, more often than not, causes issues that could otherwise have been avoided with proper advance planning.

Potential Delays in the Process

Because of the inherent legal and procedural complexities of the purchase and sale of real estate, it is not at all uncommon to experience delays. Anticipating common delays will help keep the transaction on schedule or at least minimize the duration of the delay.

Buyer Loan Commitment and Disclosure

If the buyer is applying for mortgage financing their obligation to purchase will likely be contingent upon their mortgage lender agreeing to finance your particular property. It will also be dependent on the buyer's continued qualification and their ability to meet certain conditions set by the lender. The buyer's option to withdraw from the transaction based on financing issues should be limited to a certain date. That date needs to be detailed in the purchase contract and is usually 14 to 20 days, or more, prior to the closing date.

If the buyer is unable to get a financing commitment from their lender before the contingency date, the buyer may request an extension of that date, or request the return of their deposit. Agreeing to an extension could mean that the closing date will also likely change. The seller should plan accordingly, particularly if the seller has their own purchase subsequent to the sale.

Recently imposed federal lending regulations known as the Truth in Lending, Real Estate Settlement Procedures Act Integrated Disclosure rule, or" TRID" for short can add significant, unexpected delays to the closing.

Sellers need to be prepared in the event their buyer is unable to perform on the closing date due to compliance with the new TRID rules. Under the rules the buyer's lender is obligated to provide the buyer with certain notices and disclosures. If the disclosures are not provided in time, or need to be provided again the buyer cannot close until the disclosures are received on accordance with the rule. Changes in the disclosure process are frustrating, and often out of the buyer's control. Unfortunately, sellers are also adversely affected by these delays and they should be aware of the potential and plan accordingly.

Plot Plan Survey

A plot plan exam or mortgage survey is an inspection of the apparent property lines based on municipal and registry of deed records. The basic intent of the survey is to determine that the foundation of the property sits within the boundary lines and that no other critical structures encroach onto or off of the property. The survey may identify zoning setbacks and flood zone related issues. If the survey discloses issues, the seller will need to address them prior to closing.

Pest Inspection

Often lenders expect the buyer to obtain a professional pest inspection as part of their application. The inspection will disclose the presence of pests and possibly damage caused by pests such as termites or carpenter ants. If pests or damage are discovered, the seller may be asked to treat and repair prior to closing.

Ignoring Agent's Advise

Sellers often make a number of other mistakes that hurt their ability to sell their property, but the worst thing they can do is to ignore the advice of their real estate agent or attorney. If the agent suggests they take specific action prior to closing and the seller either ignores the advice or does something contrary or improperly, the seller's actions may cause needless delays in the closing. For example, if you overprice the property, and still manage to find a buyer who is willing to match the price, a bank appraisal of the property may reveal that the property is overpriced, and the bank may refuse to lend the buyer enough to purchase the property. In such a case, either the price has to be renegotiated or the buyer will be forced to walk away altogether, despite being willing to pay the higher than market price. However, in rare circumstances the buyer may be willing to pay more than the appraised value, and may be able to do so if the mortgage lender also agrees, but these instances are extremely rare.

Avoiding Last Minute Problems

When I represent a seller as a real estate attorney, I take them through a standard checklist of questions, including whether or not they pay child support, have filed bankruptcy or if they have any creditors who are trying to collect. If they answer "yes," I go a step further and see if there may be a potential lien against the property or other circumstances that may impact the sale. Going through this review process in advance is critical in avoiding delays and identifying potential concerns.

The closing attorney, as part of the closing process, will examine the title and note liens and mortgages that must be paid off or discharged. If there is a lien on the property or other title issue, it should be discovered well before the closing date to avoid any possible delays. However, there are attorneys who may not practice real estate enough or don't practice it well. Often, they don't get their title reports done until two or three days prior to closing, which means that if and when the seller finds out there is a problem with title, such as a lien or a more serious title defect, it can lead to problems in the transaction and prevent the transaction from closing on time.

Follow up with the closing attorney early on, provide them with information they request, and encourage them to complete the tile exam sooner than later.

Common Issues with Property Titles

The most common cloud or defect found in a title is an un-discharged mortgage from one of the previous owners. When a person buys a piece of property from a seller, at the closing, that seller's current mortgage is paid off and released from the record of title. Although the mortgage would have been paid off at the purchase closing, for whatever reason, it was never released from the chain of title. So the entire time the person owned the property, the previous mortgage was still apparently in effect, at least in terms of still appearing on record as active.

More often than not, such an event happens when a lender was paid off in the chain of title, but the previous owner failed to send the appropriate documentation to the registry of deeds. If that information is not removed from the public record, it shows that the mortgage is outstanding and valid. To rectify an error such as this, the seller or their attorney would have to get in touch with the mortgage company that was paid off, and get them to acknowledge, in writing, that the mortgage was indeed paid and should be removed from the chain of ownership. Once acknowledged, it will then be recorded at the registry of deeds and the discrepancy would be cleared up.

Another common issue would be that of an error in the description of the property contained in a deed in the chain of title. Often, it is an error in the current deed where only a portion of the property was conveyed, or the wrong property was conveyed. Issues like this can cause serious delays and are not often discovered until the completion of the exam.

Less common discrepancies can also occur – ones that are of much graver consequence that affect the chain of title, but aren't necessarily the fault of anyone involved in the transaction. For example, a situation where the deed in the chain of title that was delivered after the death of the property's current owner, such as, someone who may have gotten the property from a parent through inheritance. Picture a scenario where a father wants to transfer a property deed to his son. So he fills out the deed, signs it, has it notarized and he intends to convey the title of the property to his son. However, for whatever reason, he takes that deed and puts it in a desk drawer and never actually manages to give the deed to his son.

A few days later, he passes away and the son goes through his father's belongings and finds the deed. The son then takes the deed to the registry of deeds and records it. However, the deed is no longer valid after the death of the current owner. In Massachusetts and many other states, a deed delivered after death is considered invalid.

The son may believe that he now has clear ownership of the property, which would also appear that way in the registry records. However, when an examiner goes through the records, they will discover that the father did, in fact, grant title to the son, and that it appears to be a good, clear title. Unfortunately, if at a later time, it can be proven that the deed was indeed delivered after death, the deed would be rendered invalid and each of the subsequent conveyance of ownership after that would also be invalidated. Such an occurrence is not particularly common, but it has been known to happen.

Title Insurance for a Property in Massachusetts

Title insurance is an insurance policy that reimburses a property owner for situations as extreme as a deed being delivered after death, for an issue as simple as a missing or unrecorded document or for a discrepancy in the deed. In some cases, a title insurance claim is just a matter of the insurer paying to obtain a discharge for the prior owner's mortgage. However, in some cases, a person may be completely divested of their ownership of the property, which would be the worst case scenario, but it has been known to happen, albeit, infrequently. The title insurance policy would cover the beneficiary's losses in such instances.

The title insurance will only insure the beneficiary of the policy, which is why it is advised to purchase an owner's policy of title insurance whenever you purchase any property. A property owner is never covered under a lender's title insurance policy. A seller should find out in advance of listing the property for sale if they have an owner's title insurance policy. Knowing this early on will help speed up resolution of many, but not all, title issues. The title insurance policy would have been purchased at the time of the closing and its details may be found with closing documentation the seller may have received at their purchase closing.

Smoke and Carbon Monoxide Detectors

Massachusetts general law (Chapter 148, Section 26E) requires residential properties to be inspected by the local fire department for compliance with the state's smoke alarm regulations upon the sale of the property. It is commonly the seller's responsibility to arrange for the inspection and to obtain the required certificate showing compliance with the law. More often than not the seller's real estate agent will coordinate the process for the seller. However, in circumstances where there is no listing agent, or where the agent does not make the arrangements, this requirement can be overlooked. Not having the certificate available in time for closing will cause delays. Municipalities have their own set of regulations or ordnances with regard to the state law. It can be very expensive to bring a property into compliance with these regulations. This expense should be considered prior to listing a home for sale.

Condominium Certificates

If the property being sold is a condominium unit, the seller is required to obtain a "6 (d) Certificate" from the condominium management. This is the certificate necessary to prove that all of the fees due to the association for the common area expenses for the property are current and paid in full. If the seller is not current with the payments, the fees will have to be collected from the seller and paid at the closing. Fees for the current month should be adjusted between the buyer and seller at closing. Failing to make arrangements to obtain the certificate in time for closing will result in a delay.

Septic Systems and Title 5

There are a number of reasons why transactions can take longer to close; one of the biggest issues that can delay a closing involves septic system compliance. In Massachusetts, Title 5 is the state regulation governing all septic systems in Massachusetts. The Department of Environmental Protection works in conjunction with municipal Boards of Health, and is responsible for enforcing the Title 5 Code. Generally, the seller is responsible for making sure that the property is inspected prior to closing and to ensure that the system is functioning properly. An inspection of the system in accordance with Title 5 should take place prior to listing the property for sale. By inspecting the system in advance, a seller will know up front if there are any issues that might delay the closing process. A system that does not pass the inspection may take up to a few weeks in order to complete the repairs. Moreover, other factors such as, the weather, also effect the time it may take to close the deal. Since there is a cost to have the system inspected and because most inspections are only valid for a period of two years, some sellers, in order to save money and time, wait until just before closing to have the inspection. This can often lead to the seller finding out at the last minute that the system needs to be repaired or replaced. And this can be very costly and time consuming, as it has the potential to hold up the transaction for an extended period of time.

Early and Truthful Disclosure

Throughout my practice as a real estate attorney, I've asked sellers if they had ever filed for bankruptcy. Most usually tell me they haven't. However, there have been cases where I had to find out the hard way, at the last minute, a few days before closing, resulting in a delay that could have easily been avoided.

It is important for sellers to realize that their attorney is working towards their best interests. It is vital for you to be completely transparent and accurate with both, your real estate agent and the attorney, for them to be able to adequately perform their job, which is to facilitate your real estate transaction without any problems. Do not provide your attorney or agent with false, incorrect or incomplete information. Doing so more often than not, in my experience, only leads to problems and delays.

As we have discussed, your attorney and agent are working to protect your best interests, concealing potential issues with your property will only put you at a disadvantage at a later date. And it will likely lead to potentially costly delays and other issues. If you are aware of any easements, environmental or use restriction or agreements, written or not, which ultimately affect the property you are trying to sell, it is prudent to disclose this information up front to your agent or attorney. This includes anything that might cause your property to be subject to affordable housing restrictions, or rights of first refusal.

Vacating the Premises

Commonly when signing the purchase and sale agreement, the seller agrees to vacate the property and deliver access to the buyer on a specific date. It is important to understand the timing of this is critical to the buyer. If the seller does not vacate and deliver the property as agreed, it constitutes a breach of contract.

Such scenarios tend to happen on occasions, as sometimes a seller has been on the property for over 25-30 years and they take their time vacating, rather than doing it as quickly as they should. There could be a number of reasons why this happens, it may be that, they didn't have enough time to properly vacate the property, or they are emotionally attached and just don't want to rush out. Whatever the case may be, needless procrastination has known to adversely affect the transaction and the closing.

Unless other arrangements or understanding has been made and agreed upon in writing, a seller is contractually obligated to vacate the property by the date of closing. This means that the seller must be completely moved out along with all of their personal property. So it is wise to plan in advance where to relocate after you close on the sale.

Removal of Fixtures

Then there is the issue of sellers taking things from the property they legally shouldn't be taking, and especially anything that can be considered as a fixture of the home. For example, just before closing, a seller may decide to take a chandelier out of the dining room because it has been in the family for 30 years and they have always moved it from house to house whenever they changed homes. And then they replace it with a chandelier that, they bought at a big box store for $20. Something like this is a clear breach of the contract because fixtures are considered as part of the property. In such a case, the buyer can make the argument that the seller has breached their contract by removing a fixture without the knowledge of the new owners.

From experience, I always ask my seller clients upfront if there is anything they don't consider a fixture that a buyer might otherwise consider to be a fixture – things that they would like to take with them. In the case they do say yes, the item should be removed before a potential buyer sees the property. If the buyer has already seen the property, the item needs to be clearly excluded as part of the sale in the purchase and sale contract.

As a general rule-of-thumb, I tell my clients that anything that would require a hammer or a screwdriver to detach from the property should be considered a fixture. If not, then it is considered personal property and should be removed from the property by time of the closing, unless otherwise agreed in writing.

Leaving Items Behind

Conversely, when it comes to leaving items behind, just about any item of personal property that is not in the contract needs to be taken off the property. You can't just leave your personal items behind! Most sale contracts require the property to be "broom clean" and free of debris.

For example, I had a seller, who, when purchased a property, found an old boiler in the basement. A big, heavy cast iron boiler that was extremely difficult to move. The owner of the property then, had a newer, more efficient furnace installed to heat the home, so the old furnace was simply abandoned in its place. The buyer at that time and now my current seller client didn't particularly have any concern regarding the old furnace, since he was not planning to use the basement anyway.

A few years go by and he decides to sell the property. The new buyer performs a walkthrough of the property just before closing and notices the huge old boiler, still lounging in the basement, sitting right next to a new and modern furnace. The issue of disposing off the old boiler was never addressed prior to this event. Hence, at the closing, the seller told the buyer that the old boiler was already there when he bought the property and he planned to leave it there, even though, technically, as soon as it was separated from the property, replaced by the new furnace, it became personal property.

The terms of the contract said the seller had to remove all of personal property off the premises in time for closing. So the seller was then forced to hire someone to professionally remove it from the property and dispose of it. An additional cost of the removal was not expected by the seller, which also resulted in the delay of the closing, which could have been easily avoided had the seller known about his contractual agreement.

Solar Power

If the home you are selling has solar panels you will need to provide your Realtor® and any perspective buyer with detailed information about the system.

A buyer will need to know in advance if you own the panels or if you are leasing them from a solar or utility company. This will make a big difference in their value and any possible complications that may arise prior to closing.

If you own the panels are owned, the value of the panels should be factored into the asking price of the home. Speak with your Realtor® about other homes in your market with panels and that are similar to the home you are selling to determine if the value of the panels on the home is reasonable.

Many solar panel systems, whether leased or owned have the benefit of the value of Solar Renewable Energy Credits (SREC). Panels generate SREC credits and someone is likely receiving the benefit/value of these credits. Every megawatt hour (MWh) of electricity produced by the solar panel system generates an SREC. Utility companies purchase these credits in order to comply with Federal renewable energy mandates. So, the property may benefit from both the electricity generated by the solar array, and by the SREC it generates. However, sometimes, a property owner only receives the benefit of the electricity, and the solar company retains the rights to the value of the SRECs.

Buyers need to understand how they will benefit from the panels. Every system is different, some arrays produce more power than others, some are leased, some are owned outright, and contract terms and conditions vary greatly from one solar vendor to another. Have the particular details of your system and your solar power purchase contract available for review. If you plan to retain any beneficial interest in the solar panels or the contract (SRECs) after closing, the buyer needs to be made aware of this and a separate contract covering the terms needs to be entered into.

Conclusion

As you probably understand by now, a real estate transaction is a complicated process that requires the involvement and participation of experienced and professional supervision. Planning for delays in advance is a must. Don't try to base your schedule entirely around the obligations and expected conduct of the buyer. When the parties set high expectations of each other, and those expectations are not met, it often leads to undue stress, rash decisions and impulsive actions.

Be sure to have a backup plan, a contingency of sorts, in the event the buyer is not prepared to close on time, or in the event of some other delay. Having a contingency plan is not always possible, but if you are able to make accommodations in advance for delays, you will be better prepared to react to the delay.

David R. Rocheford, Jr.

has been involved in real estate for over 20 years. First as a real estate agent while attending college at night. Later David worked as a paralegal and as an intern for a busy real estate law office while attending law school.

After graduating, David started his own practice and dedicated himself to becoming an expert in real estate matters. He has been involved in well over 7,000 real estate transactions and his practices represents banks, mortgage lenders, buyers and sellers. Having experienced firsthand the common mistakes that adversely affect his seller clients, this book is intended to help home sellers recognize some of the mistakes to avoid.

Made in the USA
Middletown, DE
24 November 2021